Violin
Scales
and
Positions

KEITH COOK

authorHOUSE®

AuthorHouse™
1663 Liberty Drive
Bloomington, IN 47403
www.authorhouse.com
Phone: 1 (800) 839-8640

Published by AuthorHouse 08/21/2019

ISBN: 978-1-7283-2366-4 (sc)
ISBN: 978-1-7283-2365-7 (e)

Library of Congress Control Number: 2019912159

Print information available on the last page.

*Any people depicted in stock imagery provided by Getty Images are models,
and such images are being used for illustrative purposes only.
Certain stock imagery © Getty Images.*

This book is printed on acid-free paper.

CONTENTS

Note: While it is understood that the use of accidentals and words together is redundant, this is done to train the young student to say the word "sharp" or "flat" when needed.

G Major

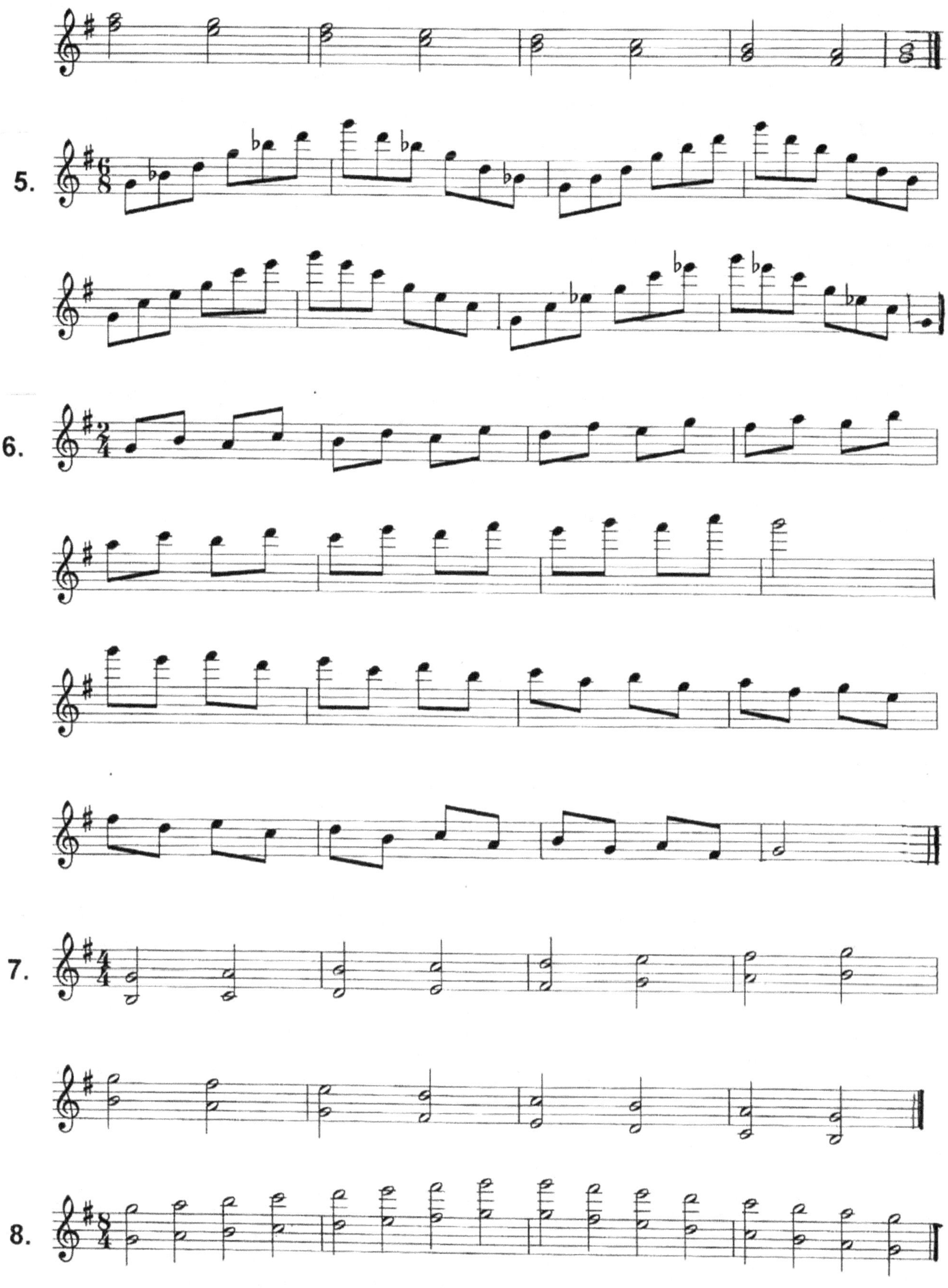
5.
6.
7.
8.

D Major

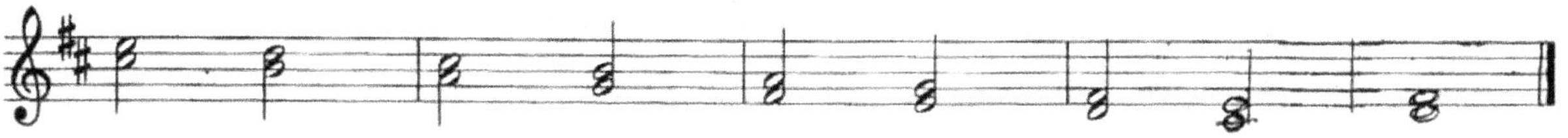

5.

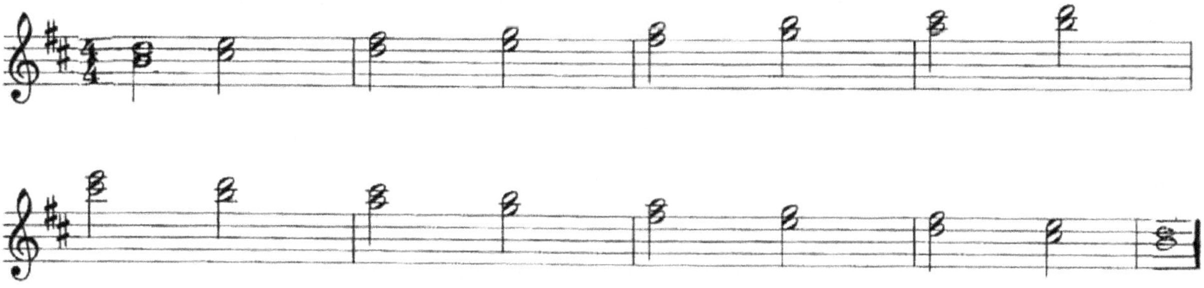

6.

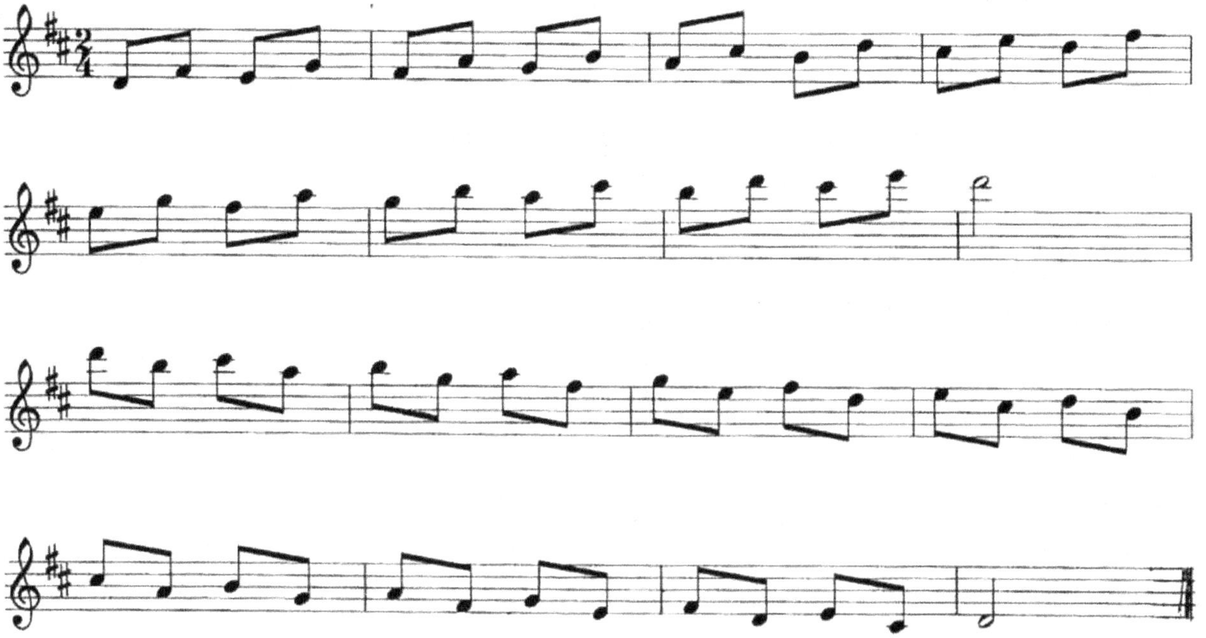

7.

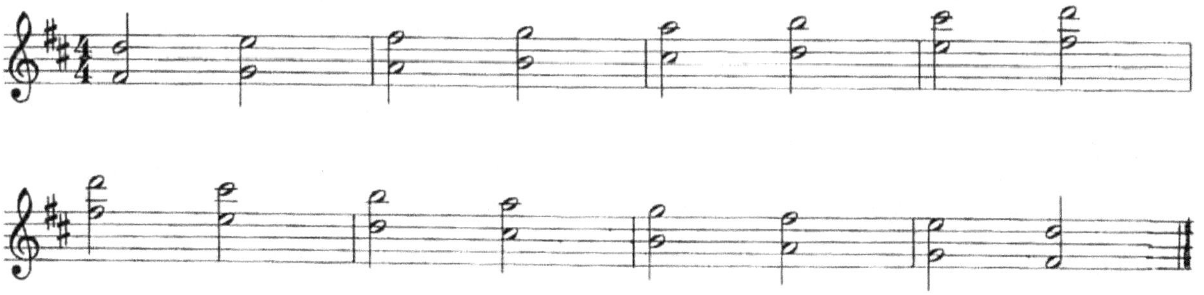

8.

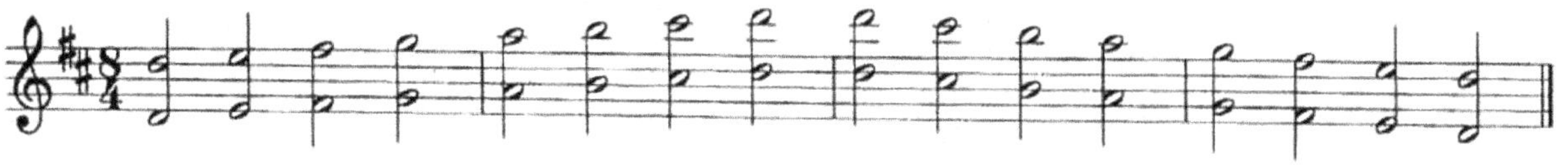

A Major

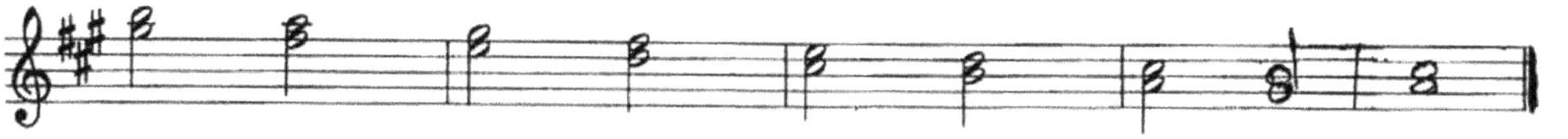

5.

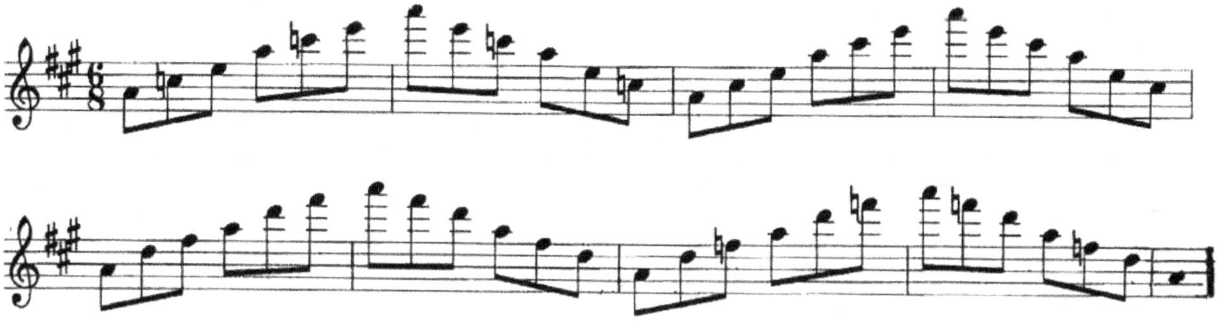

6.

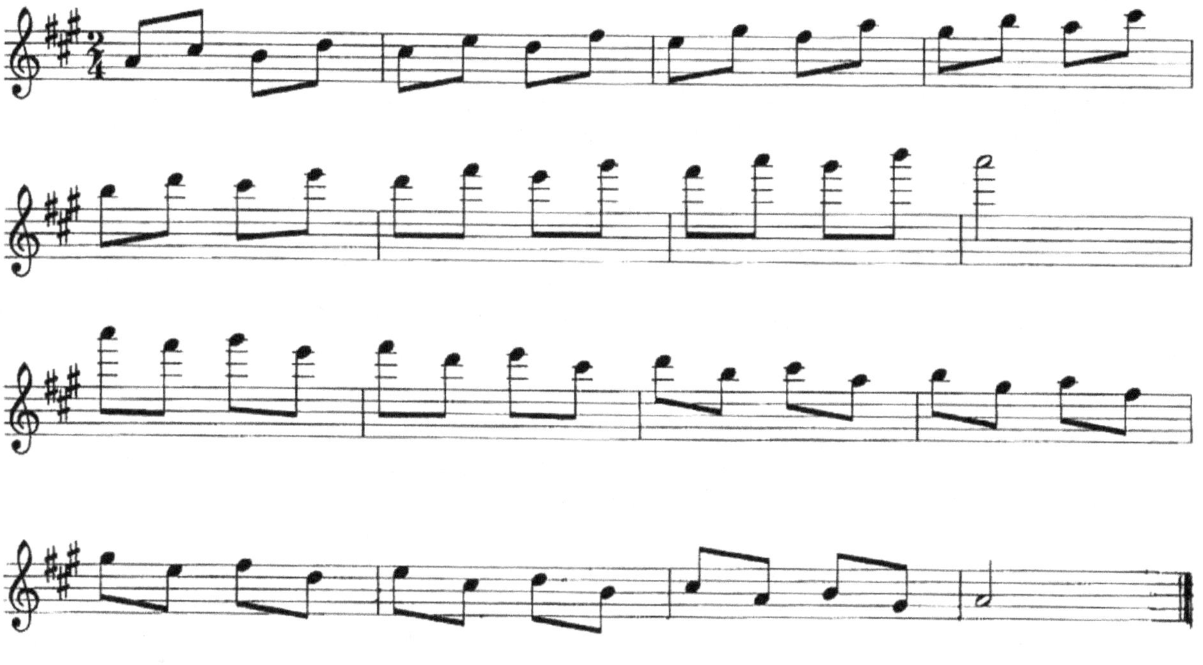

7.

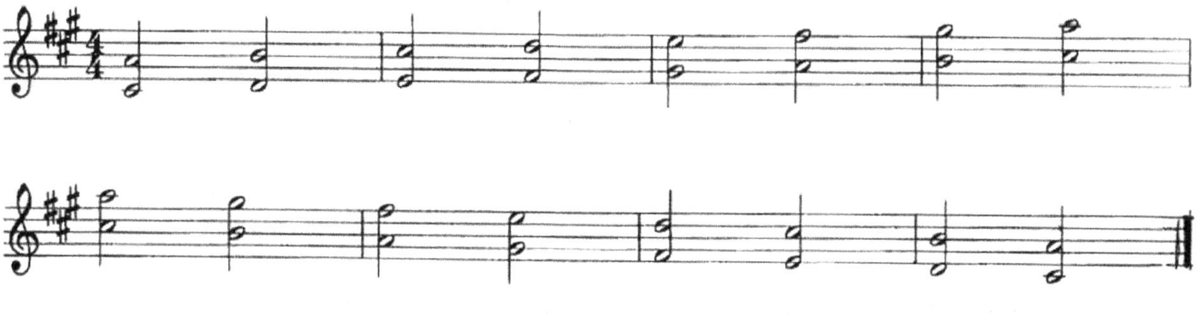

8.

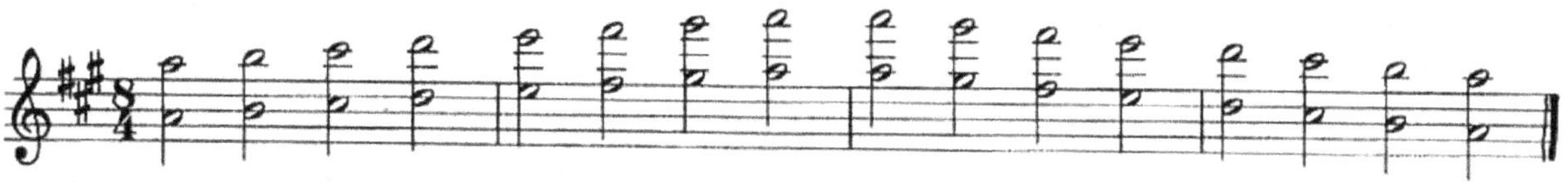

E Major

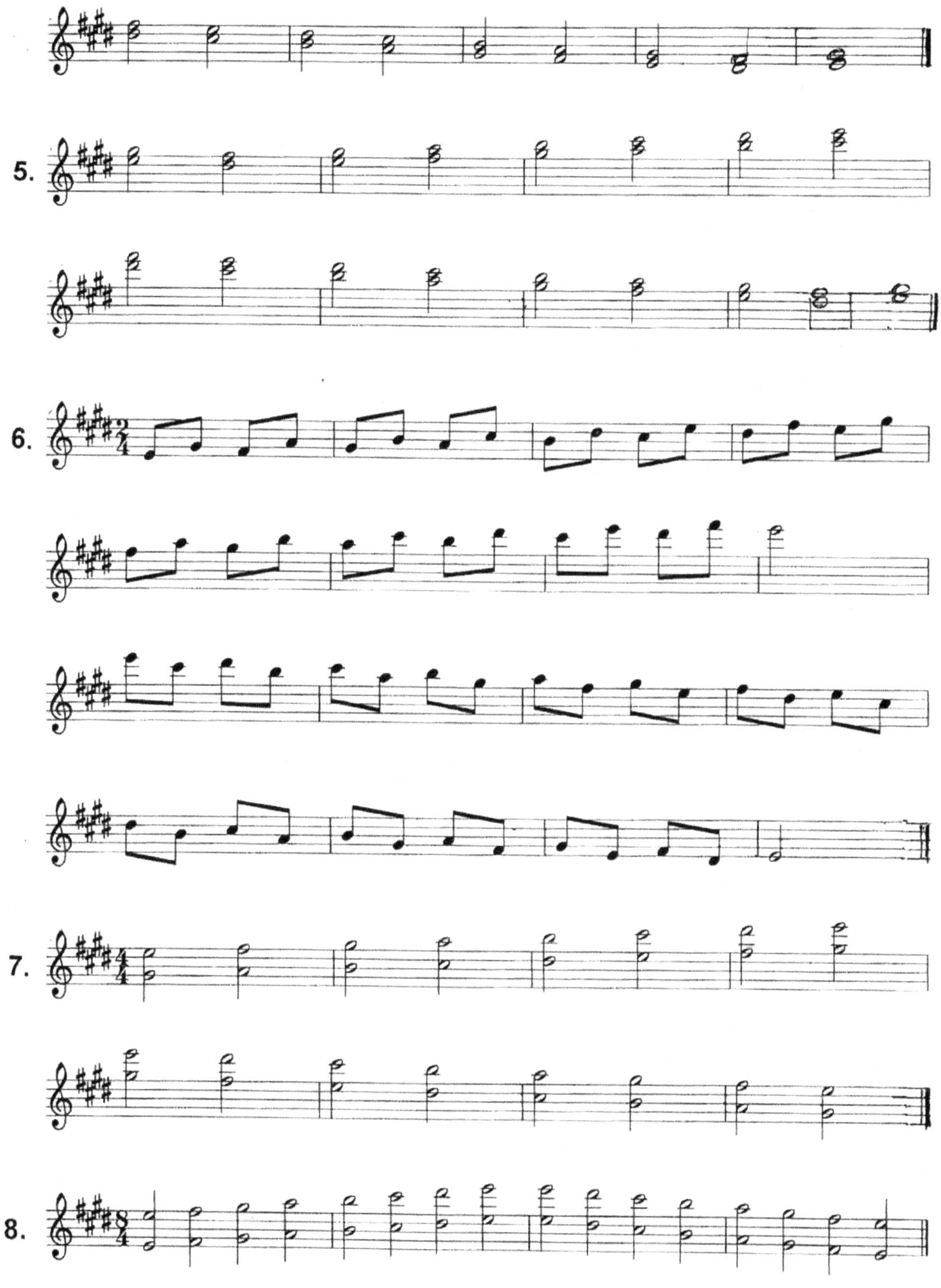
5.
6.
7.
8.

B Major

Play *March in B* by reading the bottom line. Play in first position. Then, *with the left hand still in first position*, read the top line. The notes will sound the same, but you will now be in second position.

MARCH in B

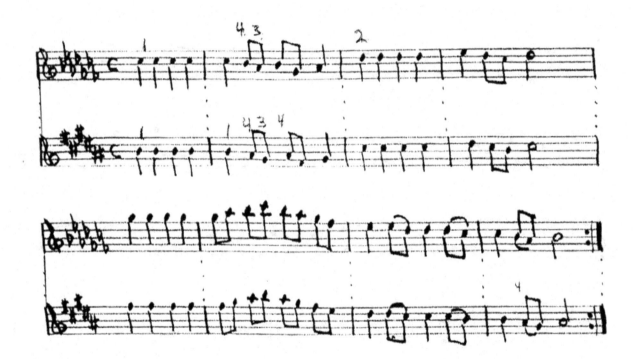

Gb flat Major / F# sharp Major

5.

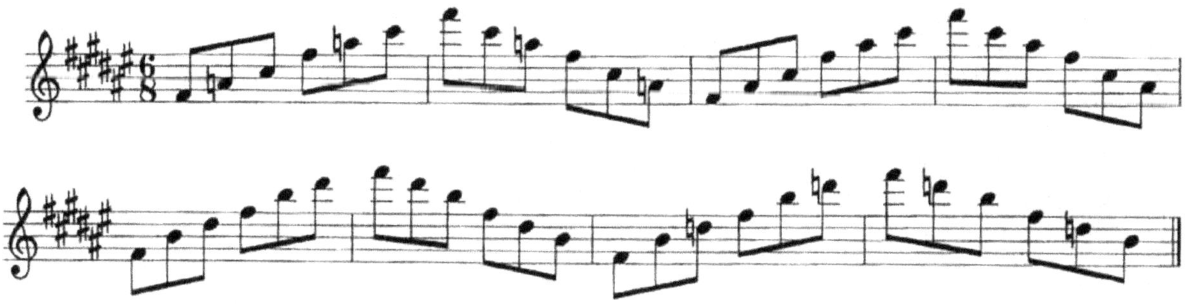

6.

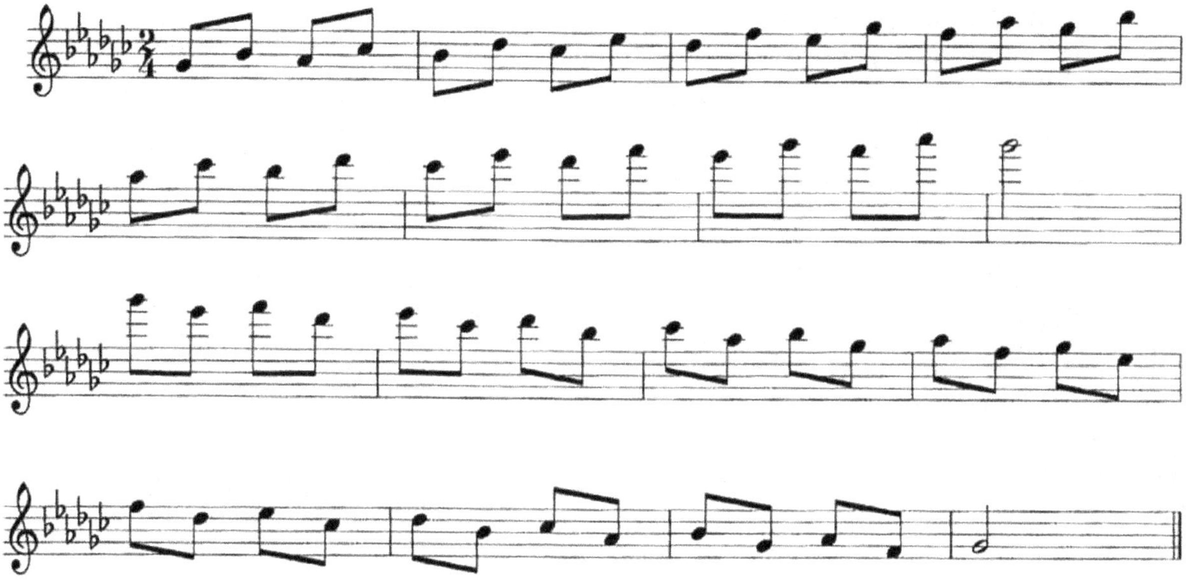

7.

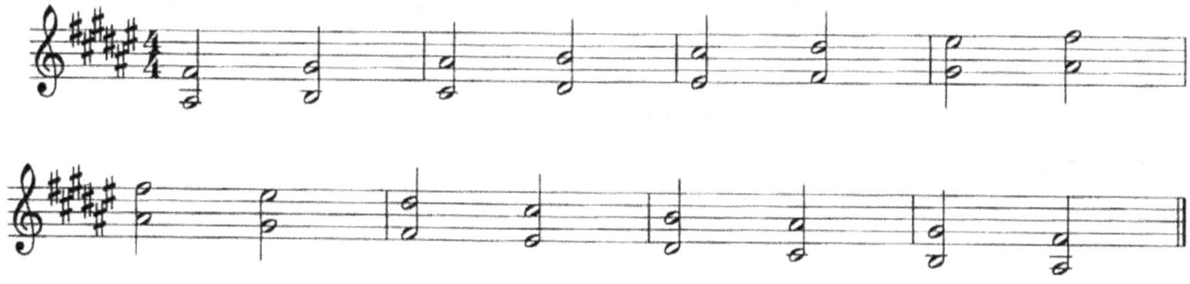

8.

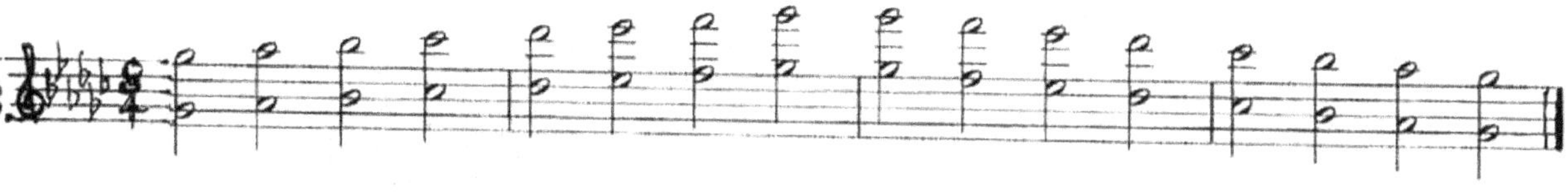

Gb flat Major / F# sharp Major

SIX FLARPS DANCE

March in B

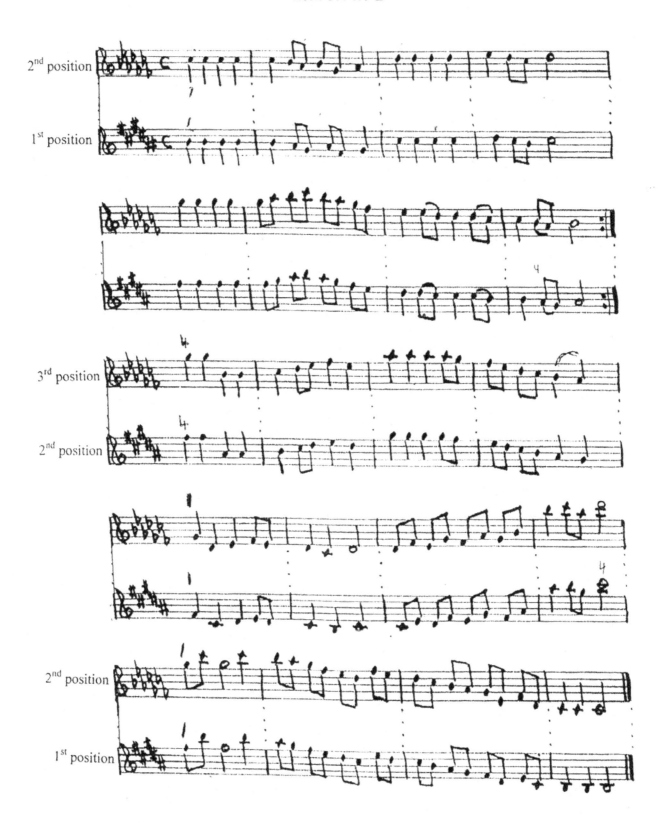

Db flat Major

Joy in D flat

Ab flat Major

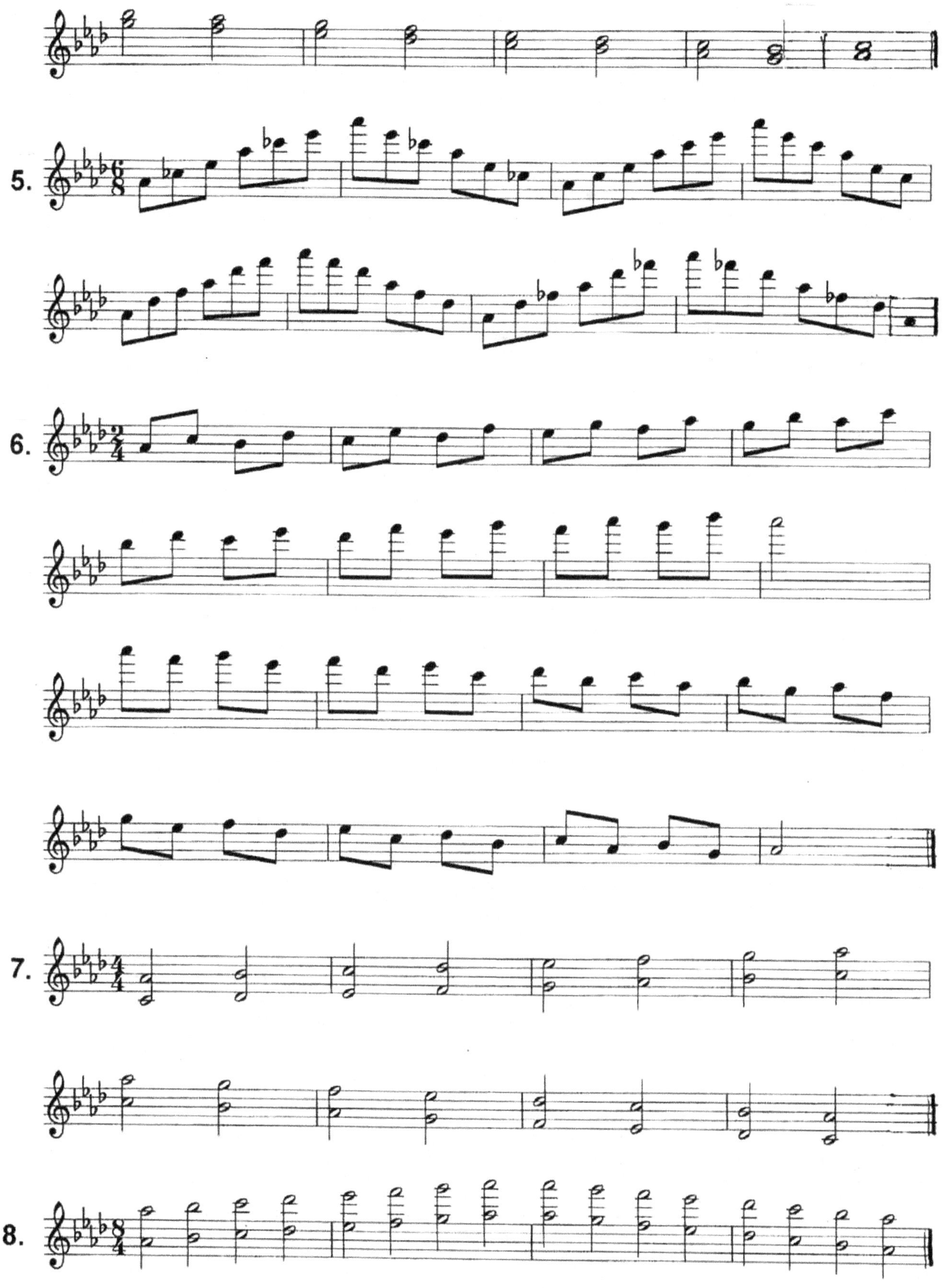
5.
6.
7.
8.

Eb flat Major

Bb flat Major

F Major

C Major

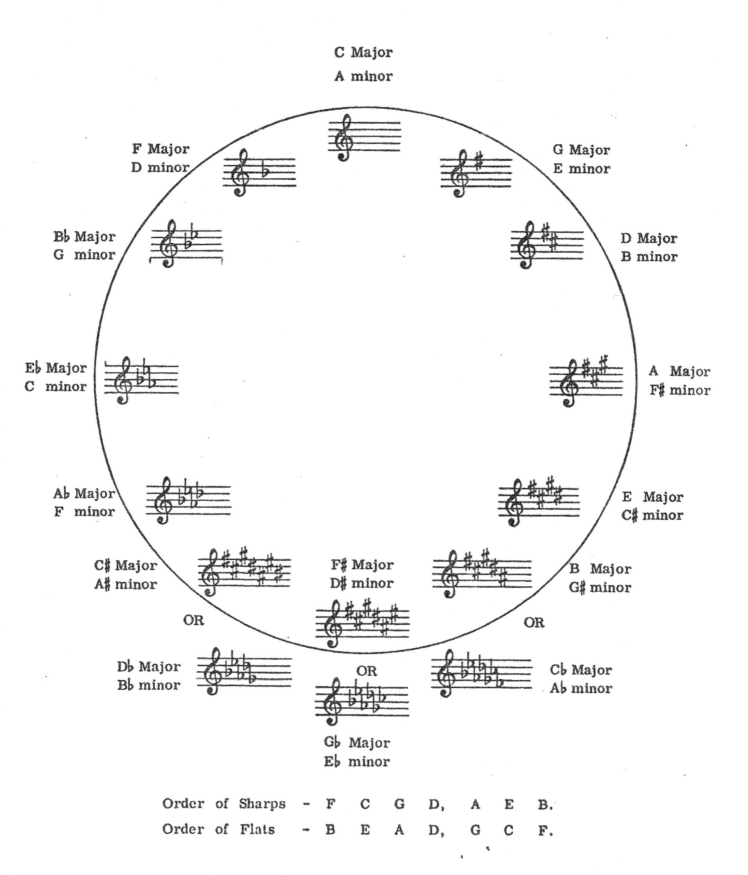

Order of Sharps — F C G D, A E B.

Order of Flats — B E A D, G C F.

A minor

D minor

G minor

C minor

F minor

Bb flat minor

Eb flat minor

D# minor

D# minor/ Eb minor

3rd position

1.

2 3 4 1

1.

4th position

2.

2.

Ab minor

Cook

G# sharp minor

C# sharp minor

F# sharp minor

B minor

E minor

Position Fingering Chart

This position fingering chart appears as a "white note" chart. Please, add accidentals as needed for each corresponding key that is not C major or A minor. For example, add the three flats to the fourth position chart when doing it in E flat major; add the four sharps when doing it in the key of E major.

The darkened notes (G2, A1 and E4) indicate the octaves defined by that position. There is also a defining set of octaves G1, D4 and E3. The upper pair of octaves is helpful to know as progress is made toward the study of three octave scales.

Eighth position is included here because it is first position, one octave higher. This is helpful to know when sight reading passages in high range.

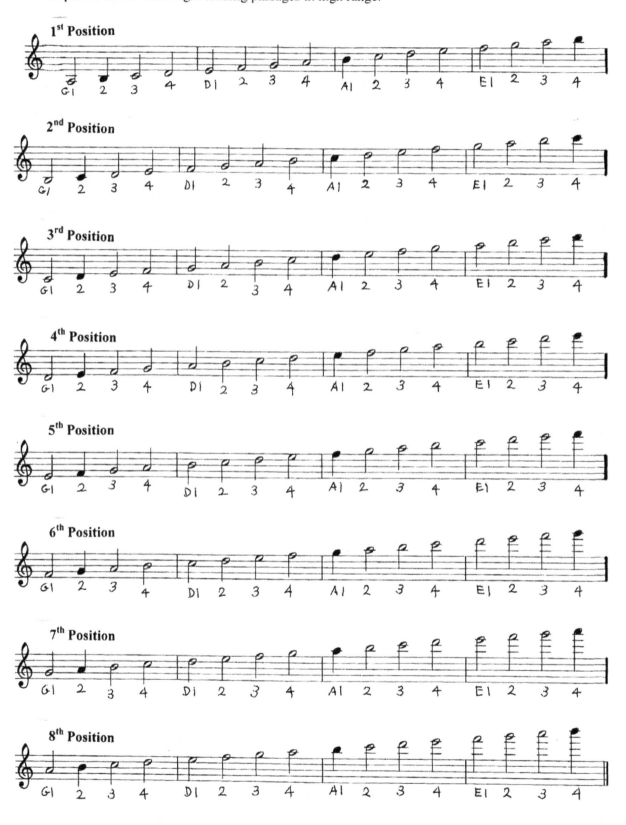